MILLION MAP

The Paths to Wealth

Edimilson Franca

CONTENTS

Title Page
Million Map: The Paths to Wealth … 1
Introduction: The Future of Wealth … 2
The Artificial Intelligence Revolution … 3
AI and Market Trend Forecasting … 4
Automation and Digital Entrepreneurship … 5
Social Media and the Power of Influencer Marketing … 6
The Role of Digital Platforms … 7
Democratization of Wealth: An Accessible Path … 8
Chapter 1: The Digital Age and the New Wealth … 9
Chapter 2: Artificial Intelligence and the Power of the Algorithm … 14
Chapter 3: Automated Business: Passive Earnings with AI … 19
Chapter 4: From Zero to Million with AI Startups … 24
Chapter 5: The Power of Digital Networking … 28
Chapter 6: Financial Education and AI: Learning Fast … 32
Chapter 7: The Impact of Cryptocurrencies and Blockchain … 36
Chapter 8: AI in the Investment World: How to Maximize Gains … 40
Chapter 9: Monetizing Skills with Digital Platforms … 44
Chapter 10: The Power of Automation in E-commerce … 49

Chapter 11: Smart Investing with AI	54
Chapter 12: AI Tools for Budding Entrepreneurs	59
Chapter 13: The Gig Economy and the New Wealth	63
Chapter 14: Tech Entrepreneurship: The Next Frontier	67
17 How AI is Revolutionizing Digital Marketing	71
1. Data Analysis and Behavior Prediction	72
2. Personalization at Scale	73
3. Real-Time Campaign Optimization	74
4. Chatbots and Automated Customer Service	75
5. Programmatic Ads with AI	76
6. The Importance of Smart SEO	77
Examples of Success with AI in Digital Marketing	78
AI as the Future of Digital Marketing	79
Chapter 16: Investing in Technological Innovations	80
Chapter 17: Experience Economy and Personalization with AI	84
Chapter 18: How Artificial Intelligence Will Reshape the Future of Wealth	89
Chapter 19: The Fastest Path to a Million: Current Strategies	94
Final Thoughts: Your Roadmap to a Million	99

MILLION MAP: THE PATHS TO WEALTH

INTRODUCTION: THE FUTURE OF WEALTH

In the 21st century, the concept of wealth is being radically redefined, driven by the convergence of new technologies, in particular, Artificial Intelligence (AI), social networks and digital platforms. The digital revolution has not only accelerated the way money is generated and accumulated, but it has also democratized the process of creating wealth, offering opportunities that were previously reserved only for a financial elite. In this scenario, any individual with access to the correct tools and adequate knowledge can embark on the path to financial success, even starting from scratch.

THE ARTIFICIAL INTELLIGENCE REVOLUTION

Artificial Intelligence, which has already infiltrated almost every aspect of our lives, is playing a central role in the new era of wealth creation. To understand the impact of AI on the economy, it is crucial that we recognize how it has been transforming the market, from automating processes to predicting trends with unprecedented accuracy.

AI's ability to process and analyze vast amounts of data in an incredibly short time has revolutionized the way financial decisions are made. In the past, to make a strategic decision, it was necessary to rely on time-consuming human analysis, often based on subjective interpretations. Today, with AI, algorithms can comb through thousands of financial reports, analyze market fluctuations and even predict changes before they are even noticeable to the human eye. This power allows investors and entrepreneurs to make faster and more effective decisions, avoiding mistakes that could be catastrophic in times of volatility.

AI AND MARKET TREND FORECASTING

One of the biggest attractions of AI is its ability to predict trends. With machine learning, AI analyzes historical patterns and, unlike humans, it is able to learn from data in real time, adjusting its predictions as the market evolves. This type of predictive analysis is becoming an essential tool for investors and companies looking to anticipate economic changes and identify promising sectors before they become apparent to the majority.

For example, AI algorithms are being used in the stock market to identify buying and selling patterns that precede significant changes in stock prices. By integrating these algorithms into automated trading systems, investors are able to execute transactions in fractions of a second, taking advantage of minimal market fluctuations. Some of the modern millionaires, such as hedge fund managers and high-frequency traders, have built their fortunes using these AI-based automated systems.

AUTOMATION AND DIGITAL ENTREPRENEURSHIP

In addition to its ability to predict trends, AI is boosting digital entrepreneurship, automating tasks that previously consumed a large part of entrepreneurs' time and resources. Today, AI-based tools can manage everything from customer service to personalized marketing campaigns, allowing individual entrepreneurs or small businesses to operate with the efficiency of large corporations.

Platforms like Shopify and Amazon, for example, already offer integrated AI solutions that automate sales processes, from product recommendations to after-sales service. AI also facilitates inventory management, price optimization and consumer behavior analysis, enabling companies to offer a personalized experience to each customer without the need for a massive support team.

In the world of digital business, this automation reduces operational costs and, more importantly, frees up entrepreneurs' time so they can focus on innovation and growing their businesses. It's no surprise, then, that many of the new millionaires are digital entrepreneurs who have managed to scale their businesses quickly using AI.

SOCIAL MEDIA AND THE POWER OF INFLUENCER MARKETING

In addition to AI, social media plays a crucial role in the modern wealth landscape. They not only connect billions of people around the world, but they also create unprecedented opportunities for building personal brands and companies. The phenomenon of digital influencers is a clear example of this. By building large audiences on platforms like Instagram, YouTube and TikTok, everyday individuals are becoming millionaires, capitalizing on their popularity through brand partnerships and direct product sales.

Influencer marketing, driven by AI algorithms that identify and recommend relevant content to users, is one of the most profitable areas of digital marketing today. Brands use AI to analyze behavioral data and predict which influencers will have the greatest impact on their campaigns, while influencers themselves use AI tools to optimize their posts and maximize their reach. This is a cycle that benefits both companies and individuals, creating a new class of digital millionaires.

THE ROLE OF DIGITAL PLATFORMS

Digital platforms like YouTube, TikTok, and even blogs monetized through Google AdSense, offer a clear and accessible path to generating wealth. Anyone with a cell phone camera and an innovative idea can create content that, when combined with the right AI strategies for viewability optimization, can reach millions of people. Thus, these platforms create an environment where creativity can be monetized in an extremely profitable way, as evidenced by countless content creators who have managed to turn their hobby into a multi-million dollar career.

Additionally, AI is also being used to personalize the user experience on these platforms by recommending content that is more likely to appeal to the target audience. This significantly increases content creators' chances of success as their videos, articles or posts are directly presented to the most suitable audience.

DEMOCRATIZATION OF WEALTH: AN ACCESSIBLE PATH

The combination of AI, social networks and digital platforms is leveling the playing field, allowing anyone, regardless of their background or background, the opportunity to create wealth. What was once an arduous path reserved for a small elite with access to capital, is now available to everyone who has an innovative idea and the willingness to use these modern tools.

Artificial Intelligence, in particular, makes the process of creating wealth more accessible and predictable. With the right tools, anyone can start investing, building an online business, or even creating content with a global impact, always supported by algorithms that offer powerful insights and automation that makes business management easier.

AI, social networks and digital platforms are transforming the way wealth is generated and distributed in the modern world. These innovations not only create new millionaires, but also open the door to an unprecedented democratization of wealth. The future of wealth belongs to those who know how to use these tools to innovate, automate and create value in an increasingly connected and data-driven world.

CHAPTER 1: THE DIGITAL AGE AND THE NEW WEALTH

Introduction to the Digital Age and Its Implications

The advent of the digital era has brought an unprecedented revolution in the way money is generated, accumulated and distributed in the world. This transformation profoundly altered the rules of the financial game, allowing companies and individuals to create wealth at a speed and scale never before seen. The emergence of giants like Google, Amazon, and a myriad of Artificial Intelligence (AI)-based startups clearly illustrates how the modern digital environment has redefined the paths to becoming a millionaire.

What distinguishes the digital age from previous eras is its accessibility. In the past, wealth creation was often restricted to wealthy families, traditional industries and power networks. With the internet and digital technologies, anyone with a computer and an internet connection can, theoretically, build a financial empire. The democratization of information and the proliferation of technological tools have given rise to a new class of millionaires who thrive in the digital economy, where innovation and rapid adaptation are the main competitive differentiators.

The Rules of the Financial Game in the Digital Age

The global economy has undergone a significant transition. Instead of being predominantly based on tangible assets such as land and factories, wealth is now largely generated by intangible assets such as data, algorithms and intellectual property. This new environment has changed the way financial success is achieved.

First, barriers to entry have decreased dramatically. To start a digital business, a modern entrepreneur needs much less initial capital than a traditional entrepreneur from the last century. This is due to the scalable nature of digital businesses, where online platforms, such as software marketplaces and social networks, allow an innovative idea to reach millions of people in a matter of days, without the need for large investments in physical infrastructure.

Furthermore, global digitalization has accelerated the pace of business. The speed at which financial transactions occur, market trends change and technological innovations emerge is unparalleled. The globalization of markets, driven by the internet, means that business opportunities are no longer confined to geographic borders. An entrepreneur can launch an app in a small country and, if successful, quickly expand it to a global market.

Google and the Power of Data

One of the most iconic examples of how the digital age has transformed the wealth landscape is Google. Founded in 1998 by Larry Page and Sergey Brin, Google quickly became the internet's dominant search engine and, later, one of the largest companies in the world in terms of market value.

Google's success lies not only in its ability to organize and deliver information, but also in its unique approach to data monetization. Google's advertising-based business model, powered by AI algorithms that personalize ads according to user behavior, has redefined digital marketing.

By collecting and analyzing data from billions of people around the world, Google was able to create a powerful wealth-generating engine.

Today, data is considered the "new oil", and companies that can transform large volumes of information into actionable insights are leading the race for wealth in the digital age. Google exemplifies how a technology-based company can exploit this new currency — data — to accumulate wealth while creating value for millions of users.

Amazon and the Digital Commerce Revolution

Another giant of the digital era that has transformed wealth creation is Amazon. Founded in 1994 by Jeff Bezos, the company started as a simple online bookstore and, over time, expanded to become the largest marketplace in the world. Today, Amazon sells everything from electronics to fresh food, and even hosts businesses through its cloud computing platform, Amazon Web Services (AWS).

The rise of Amazon illustrates how digital companies can thrive in a globalized environment. One of Bezos's greatest innovations was realizing that, by creating a platform where anyone could sell products, he could transform Amazon into a "virtual mall" that would serve millions of consumers around the world.

Another key aspect of Amazon's success is its commitment to continuous innovation. The company uses AI extensively to optimize its operations, from recommending personalized products for customers to automating its distribution centers. The combination of a vast network of suppliers, global consumers and cutting-edge technology has made Amazon a wealth-generating machine, both for the company itself and for the entrepreneurs who use its platform.

AI-Based Startups and the New Frontier of Wealth

While giants like Google and Amazon dominate the digital age landscape, AI-based startups are emerging as the new agents of wealth creation. AI is being applied across industries, from finance to healthcare, and many of these startups are using machine learning technologies and advanced algorithms to create innovative solutions that meet the growing demands of the global economy.

A notable example is OpenAI, an AI research organization that developed the famous GPT (Generative Pretrained Transformer) model, widely used in virtual assistants, text automation and other applications that speed up business processes. Startups like these are at the forefront of the new digital economy, exploring the frontier of AI to deliver solutions that maximize efficiency and minimize operational costs.

Smaller but equally influential companies like UiPath, which develops robotic process automation (RPA) software, are also creating new millionaires by redefining the way business is run. Automation, enabled by AI, is enabling companies to optimize their operations and scale their businesses quickly, generating huge savings and increasing profit margins.

The Creation of Millionaires in the Modern Era

The combination of data, AI and accessibility to digital platforms has been the key to creating millionaires in the modern era. The success stories of entrepreneurs like Elon Musk, Jeff Bezos and Mark Zuckerberg, all technology-driven millionaires, demonstrate that the path to riches now involves a deep understanding of digital innovation and the ability to apply that knowledge in practical ways.

Contemporary millionaires no longer rely on traditional business models. Instead, they capitalize on emerging trends like using AI to personalize customer experiences, online platforms to expand your reach, and automation to efficiently scale your operations. Furthermore, many of them have built financial empires through a data-driven approach, using information to make faster and more accurate strategic decisions.

A New Game, New Rules

What we can learn from the rise of companies like Google, Amazon and AI-based startups is that the digital era has redefined the financial game. Success and wealth creation, which were previously reserved for a few, are now within the reach of anyone who understands the new rules and knows how to use them to their advantage.

Technology, particularly AI, will continue to play a crucial role in the evolution of the global market. As these innovations become increasingly accessible, the number of millionaires created by the digital economy will only grow. The key to standing out in this new environment is to always be ahead of technological trends and know how to take advantage of the opportunities that arise.

CHAPTER 2: ARTIFICIAL INTELLIGENCE AND THE POWER OF THE ALGORITHM

Introduction: The Artificial Intelligence Revolution

Artificial intelligence (AI) has been rapidly transforming the financial market and redefining the way economic decisions are made. Where investors once relied on intuition, experience and manual analysis, now algorithms and automated systems are taking a central role. AI's ability to process immense amounts of data, identify hidden patterns and execute trades in fractions of a second has become a powerful tool for investors, from large corporations to small individual traders.

High-frequency algorithms and automated trading systems are not just efficient mechanisms for financial transactions; they are also the new architects of the success of many contemporary millionaires. In this new era, those who know how to use AI tools effectively will have a clear competitive advantage in the market.

The Power of High Frequency Algorithms

High-frequency algorithms (HFT – High-Frequency Trading) are one of the most notable advances in AI in the financial market. These systems allow transactions to be carried out in milliseconds, taking advantage of the smallest price fluctuations to generate profit. By automatically identifying and executing trades based on market patterns, HFT algorithms can achieve gains that would be impossible for humans to capture manually. Large financial institutions such as Goldman Sachs and JPMorgan already rely heavily on HFT systems to maximize their profit margins.

For example, Citadel, one of the largest asset management companies in the world, uses sophisticated algorithms to carry out millions of transactions daily. This approach has revolutionized the market, allowing large volumes of trading to occur without human intervention. HFT's impact on the market is so great that it accounts for more than 50% of trading volume on some of the world's leading stock exchanges.

Automated Trading: The Path to Wealth

In addition to high-frequency algorithms, automated trading, facilitated by AI, has also become an accessible tool for individual investors. Platforms like Robinhood, eToro and Wealthfront offer access to automated investment systems that use AI to analyze market trends and automatically adjust portfolios, without the need for a human manager. These systems are powered by real-time data and can quickly adapt to market changes, minimizing risks and maximizing returns.

Many emerging millionaires in the financial market have made their fortunes by exploring these platforms and adopting automated trading strategies. For example, cryptocurrency traders, like those who invested in the Bitcoin boom, use trading robots to monitor and react to price changes, making significant profits. The ability to adjust strategies in real time, without the need for constant monitoring by the user, makes these systems ideal for investors looking to maximize their time and minimize risk.

Small Investors and AI Tools

AI is not exclusive to big players. In recent years, artificial intelligence-based tools have become accessible to small investors, allowing anyone with a brokerage account and an internet connection to use algorithms to make more informed decisions. Platforms like Betterment and Acorns use AI to personalize investment strategies based on each client's goals and risk profile.

These tools analyze historical data and market trends to automatically optimize portfolios, adjusting asset allocation in real time as market conditions change. Using AI for predictive analysis of stocks and cryptocurrencies allows smaller investors, who previously relied on expert advice or their own manual analysis, to compete with larger players in the market.

Examples of Millionaires Who Used AI

One of the most inspiring stories of someone who built his fortune using AI is that of David Siegel, co-founder of Two Sigma Investments. His company uses artificial intelligence and machine learning to create investment strategies that outperform traditional benchmarks. Siegel amassed billions of dollars by applying AI to detect complex patterns in financial markets, creating one of the most successful hedge managers in the world.

Another example is Jim Simons, founder of Renaissance Technologies, whose Medallion fund is considered the most profitable of all time. Renaissance uses complex mathematical models and AI to perform data-driven trades, having generated average annual returns of 66% between 1988 and 2018. Simons has distinguished itself as one of the world's largest fund managers by using advanced algorithms that minimize human error and capitalize on hidden trends in markets.

Furthermore, in the world of cryptocurrencies, Sam

Bankman-Fried, founder of exchange FTX, built his fortune using AI-based algorithms for arbitrage trading between different exchanges. Bankman-Fried quickly became a billionaire by identifying and exploiting inefficiencies in the global cryptocurrency market, using AI to execute trades at a speed and accuracy no human could match.

AI Democratizing Wealth

The AI revolution is also democratizing access to information and tools previously reserved for institutional investors. Today, anyone with a smartphone can access trading platforms that use AI for predictive analysis of stocks, cryptocurrencies and other assets. This accessibility is allowing a growing number of individual investors to build significant wealth without having to rely on expensive fund managers or advanced financial expertise.

Machine learning tools can analyze enormous amounts of historical data, predict trends, and suggest actions based on complex risk-reward analysis. This gives the average investor a competitive advantage that was previously out of reach, paving the way for more people to participate in global economic growth.

Artificial intelligence and algorithms are transforming the way finance works. From high-frequency algorithms to automated trading platforms for retail investors, AI offers powerful tools for those looking to create wealth in the modern environment. The impact of this technology on creating millionaires is undeniable, and the future of AI in the financial sector promises to be even more innovative and accessible.

The success stories of great investors who have used AI to accumulate fortunes are inspiring, but they are also a reminder that the real key to success lies in understanding and using these tools intelligently. AI will continue to evolve, and with it, the opportunities to become a millionaire in the digital age will also increase. The question is: are you prepared to take advantage of these opportunities?

CHAPTER 3: AUTOMATED BUSINESS: PASSIVE EARNINGS WITH AI

Introduction: The Potential of Automation in Creating Wealth

Business automation has been one of the biggest revolutions in the modern corporate world, especially with the advancement of artificial intelligence (AI). The concept of passive earnings — that is, generating revenue with minimal direct intervention — has been largely achieved through tools and technologies that allow companies to operate almost automatically. This has created unprecedented opportunities for business owners and entrepreneurs who want to build profitable businesses without the need for intense daily involvement.

With the integration of AI, sectors such as e-commerce, digital marketing, content creation and customer service began to be conducted efficiently and almost completely automated. Automation allows operations to take place 24 hours a day, seven days a week, without the physical presence of the company owner. Business models such as dropshipping, affiliate marketing and the use of chatbots are emblematic examples of how AI is transforming the business world.

Dropshipping: An Automated Business Model

Dropshipping is one of the most popular business models for those looking to create passive income without having to deal with traditional e-commerce logistics. In this system, the entrepreneur creates an online store, but does not maintain stock. When a customer places an order, the supplier ships the product directly to the end consumer. This eliminates the need for inventory management, allowing the entrepreneur to focus solely on selling.

AI has amplified the possibilities within dropshipping. With machine learning algorithms, dropshipping platforms can identify products in high demand, predict trends, and even automatically adjust prices to compete in the market. For example, tools like Oberlo and Shopify use AI to suggest trending products, saving time and increasing efficiency.

Entrepreneurs who use automated dropshipping can easily manage their stores from anywhere in the world, without having to deal directly with physical products. This not only reduces operational costs, but also frees the entrepreneur to focus on marketing and growth strategies.

Automated Content Creation: AI Producing for You

Content creation is another area that has been transformed by AI, allowing businesses to automate their digital marketing and content production strategies. Previously, creating blogs, videos, articles and social media posts was a time-consuming task and required a lot of human effort. Today, AI tools like GPT (generative pre-training transformer) can automatically generate content based on keywords and SEO algorithms.

Companies are using AI to produce optimized blog articles, email marketing campaigns and even video scripts in an automated way. Tools like Jarvis (now called Jasper AI) are examples of AI that make it easy to create personalized, relevant content without the need for human writers.

Additionally, video and social media platforms are integrating AI to create and suggest content. YouTube, for example, uses AI algorithms to optimize titles, descriptions and even thumbnail images, increasing engagement with the audience. This offers a significant advantage for digital entrepreneurs who want to grow their brands without spending time manually creating each piece of content.

Chatbots and Automation in Customer Service

One of the biggest developments in business automation is the use of chatbots for customer service. These AI-based systems can handle frequently asked questions, process orders, and even troubleshoot problems, all without human intervention. The benefit is twofold: customers get fast, accurate answers, while business owners save time and resources.

Chatbots like those developed by the company Drift, for example, are designed to simulate human conversations and can resolve complex customer support issues. Furthermore, they can be programmed to identify when a situation needs a human representative, ensuring that the customer is served in the best possible way.

In the e-commerce sector, chatbots like those offered by Facebook Messenger or WhatsApp are enabling small businesses to offer 24-hour support, increasing customer satisfaction and conversion rates. This is particularly valuable in a world where consumers demand instant responses and constant support.

AI and Automation in Internal Processes

In addition to customer-facing aspects, AI and automation are optimizing internal processes such as accounting, inventory management and even recruitment. Workflow automation tools like Zapier and Integromat allow companies to connect different applications and processes, removing the need for manual monitoring.

In the finance sector, platforms like QuickBooks use AI to organize company finances, automatically generate reports, and ensure businesses are always in compliance with tax laws. Automating routine tasks frees up time so business owners can focus on strategic growth activities.

Furthermore, AI software in recruitment, such as Workable, allows companies to identify the best talent in an automated way, using algorithms that analyze resumes, performance data and even the behavioral profile of candidates.

Successful Examples of Using Automation for Wealth

Large companies and successful entrepreneurs have intensively explored automation to increase their efficiency and maximize profits. Elon Musk, for example, uses highly automated systems in his Tesla factories, where robots manage much of the production line. This allows the company to mass produce with high precision, reducing operating costs and production time.

Another example is Jeff Bezos, whose Amazon empire is powered by a series of automations, from order processing to delivery. Amazon pioneered the use of AI to recommend products, adjust prices and predict future demand, allowing it to be one of the most valuable companies in the world.

Smaller startups are also using AI and automation to stand out. Lemonade, an AI-powered insurance company, uses bots to process claims in minutes, saving both the company and customers time and money.

The Path to Automated Wealth

Automation, powered by AI, has opened up new opportunities for entrepreneurs looking to build profitable businesses without the need to be directly involved in the day-to-day operations. From dropshipping to automated content creation and using chatbots in customer service, the options for automated businesses are vast and accessible.

Advances in technology and AI are making it easier to create passive income, and anyone, with the right tools, can take advantage of these opportunities to achieve financial success. As technology advances, the path to automated wealth will become even clearer, more accessible, and most importantly, scalable.

CHAPTER 4: FROM ZERO TO MILLION WITH AI STARTUPS

Introduction: The Power of AI Startups

In recent years, artificial intelligence (AI) startups have emerged as a powerful force, capable of transforming simple ideas into million-dollar businesses. These ventures not only respond to global demands, but also have the potential to solve complex problems that affect society. This chapter explores inspiring stories of entrepreneurs who started from scratch and built empires through AI-based innovations. Additionally, we will discuss the opportunities that exist for new entrepreneurs to enter this growing market.

Success Stories: The Path of Visionary Entrepreneurs

Success stories like **Jasper AI**, a startup that started as a small project and quickly gained popularity, are perfect examples of the potential of AI startups. Founded by a group of technology enthusiasts, the company has developed an AI-based text generation tool that simplifies the writing process. Jasper's success is attributed to its ability to solve a real problem — creating content quickly and effectively. By understanding market needs and using cutting-edge technologies, the founders were able to attract investors and, in a short time, scale the company to a significant valuation.

Another notable example is the case of **UiPath**, which started as a small startup in an underexplored market and became a leader in robotic process automation (RPA). The story of Daniel Dines, one of the co-founders, is an inspiration to many. Dines grew up in a middle-class family in Romania and, after moving to the US, realized the need for automation in companies. Through persistence and innovation, UiPath became a unicorn (a startup valued at over a billion dollars) in less than five years.

These stories demonstrate that, with the right vision and a willingness to work hard, it is possible to turn a simple idea into a successful business.

Opportunities in AI: Solving Global Problems

The AI market is full of opportunities for those who want to innovate. Global problems such as resource scarcity, climate change and public health are crying out for effective and innovative solutions. AI startups are at the forefront of this revolution, using technology to create products and services that meet these urgent needs.

An example of success in this regard is the **Zebra Medical Vision**, which uses AI to analyze medical exams and diagnose illnesses. Founded by a group of doctors and engineers, the startup emerged to improve the accuracy of medical diagnoses and reduce the cost of healthcare. Using AI in medical image analysis not only improves diagnostic effectiveness but also saves valuable time for doctors. This type of innovation not only generates profit, but also has a significant social impact.

How to Enter the AI Startup Market

For those who want to enter the AI startup market, the first step is to identify an unmet need or a problem that can be solved with technology. Healthcare, education, logistics and finance are just a few of the many industries that benefit greatly from AI. Entrepreneurs can start by carrying out market research to understand what pain points consumers are facing and how AI can be applied to solve them.

After identifying a niche, the next step is to acquire technical knowledge in AI. This could include online courses, bootcamps, or even collaborations with experts in the field. Programming and understanding machine learning concepts are fundamental to building effective solutions. Platforms like Coursera, edX and Udacity offer quality courses that can help new entrepreneurs acquire the necessary skills.

Networking and Funding: Building a Support Network

In addition to technical knowledge, building a network of contacts is vital to the success of a startup. Attending industry events, technology conferences, and hackathons can provide opportunities to make valuable connections. Networking not only opens doors to potential investors, but also allows entrepreneurs to exchange ideas and learn from the experiences of others.

To finance their startups, entrepreneurs can consider different options, such as angel investors, venture capital or crowdfunding. Searching for financing can be challenging, but presenting a clear and convincing proposal that demonstrates the potential return on investment is crucial. AI startups have attracted the attention of investors due to their disruptive potential and scalability, which makes them attractive in the market.

The Future is Bright for AI Startups

The success stories of entrepreneurs who started from scratch and became millionaires with AI startups are a testament to the potential of this technology. As more people recognize the opportunities offered by AI, the market will continue to grow and evolve. For those willing to learn, innovate and connect, the path to becoming a millionaire is more accessible than ever.

With a combination of vision, technical skills and strong community support, anyone can turn their ideas into a successful startup. The future is bright for those who dare to dream big and act with determination.

CHAPTER 5: THE POWER OF DIGITAL NETWORKING

Introduction: The Networking Revolution in the Digital Age

Nowadays, digital networking has become a fundamental tool for anyone aspiring to achieve financial success. With the advent of social networks and connection platforms such as LinkedIn, Twitter and Clubhouse, individuals have the ability to build and expand their networks quickly and effectively. These platforms offer unique opportunities for interaction and collaboration, allowing entrepreneurs, investors and professionals to exchange ideas, share knowledge and explore new business possibilities.

The power of digital networking is particularly evident in the world of millionaires. Many of them built their fortunes not only through technical skills and knowledge, but also through strategic connections they made along their paths. This chapter will explore how social networks are making it easier to build meaningful relationships and how these interactions can accelerate the path to wealth.

LinkedIn as a Professional Connection Tool

LinkedIn is the main social network aimed at the professional world, with more than 700 million users worldwide. The platform stands out as a powerful tool for networking, allowing professionals from different areas to connect and share experiences. Many millionaires recognize the importance of LinkedIn and use the platform to build relationships with other industry leaders, find mentors and discover business opportunities.

A notable example is the case of **Reid Hoffman**, co-founder of LinkedIn. Hoffman not only helped create the platform, but also leveraged his own network to boost his career as a venture capitalist. He is known for investing in promising startups like Facebook and Airbnb, and is a firm believer in the power of networking. According to Hoffman, "Connections are the new capital, and effective networking can open doors you never knew existed."

Through LinkedIn, users can join relevant groups, follow influencers and interact with industry leaders. These interactions often result in fruitful collaborations and partnerships that can lead to business growth and, eventually, wealth creation.

Twitter: The Network of Information and Opportunity

Twitter, although initially seen as a microblogging platform, has become a powerful networking tool. With its real-time nature, Twitter allows users to share news, ideas and trends instantly. Millionaires and influencers often use Twitter to connect with their followers and build meaningful relationships with other professionals.

An example is **Elon Musk**, CEO of Tesla and SpaceX, who uses Twitter to share updates about his companies and interact directly with his fans and critics. Musk is known for his quick responses and interactions with followers, which strengthens his relationship with the community and expands his influence in the industry. This visibility can lead to new business opportunities and partnerships.

The key to success on Twitter is authenticity and the ability to share valuable insights. By interacting with other professionals and participating in relevant discussions, users can position themselves as thought leaders in their fields, attracting the attention of potential investors and partners.

Clubhouse: Networking em Tempo Real

Clubhouse, a social audio platform, has emerged as a new form of digital networking. With chat rooms where users can participate in live discussions, the platform offers an interactive and engaging experience. Millionaires and entrepreneurs use Clubhouse to share experiences, discuss industry trends, and even find new talent.

An example of effective use of Clubhouse is to **Marc Andreessen**, co-founder of Andreessen Horowitz, one of Silicon Valley's most prominent venture capital firms. Andreessen frequently participates in innovation and technology breakout rooms, where he can connect with startup founders and other investors. He uses these interactions to identify new investment opportunities and strengthen his network.

Clubhouse allows users to interact directly with experts and industry leaders, offering a unique platform for real-time networking. Live conversations create a sense of urgency and authenticity, allowing participants to connect in ways that aren't possible on other social networks.

The Importance of Strategic Connections

Building a solid network of contacts is essential to achieving financial success. Strategic connections can open doors to business opportunities, investments and collaborations. Millionaires often highlight the importance of cultivating genuine relationships and investing time in meaningful interactions.

For example, **Gary Vaynerchuk**, a well-known entrepreneur and investor, often talks about how his success is largely attributed to the connections he has made throughout his career. He advises aspiring millionaires to get actively involved in their communities and look for ways to help others, as this often results in unexpected and fruitful returns.

Additionally, many millionaires recognize that social media and digital platforms are not just for self-promotion, but also for collaboration and learning. Exchanging knowledge and experiences with other professionals can lead to valuable insights that help shape successful business strategies.

The Future of Digital Networking

Digital networking has transformed the way individuals connect and build relationships. With platforms like LinkedIn, Twitter and Clubhouse, networking opportunities are more accessible than ever. Millionaires from different areas use these tools to build strategic connections that accelerate their path to riches.

As technology continues to evolve, the potential for digital networking will only increase. For those who want to achieve financial success, investing time and effort into building meaningful networks will be a crucial strategy. The power of digital networking is real, and those who take advantage of it are well positioned to thrive in an increasingly interconnected world.

CHAPTER 6: FINANCIAL EDUCATION AND AI: LEARNING FAST

Introduction: The Transformative Role of Financial Education in the Age of AI

These days, financial education is more crucial than ever. With the increasing complexity of the financial market, it is essential that individuals of all ages and backgrounds understand the basic principles of personal finance and investing. However, access to quality financial education is not always easy. This is where Artificial Intelligence (AI) comes into play, revolutionizing the way we learn about finance and investing.

Not only is AI transforming the way information is presented, it is also delivering personalized learning that adapts to individual needs. This chapter will explore how AI-based educational platforms are changing the landscape of financial education, enabling people to learn faster and make smarter financial decisions.

The AI-Accelerated Learning Revolution

AI is becoming a driving force in education, facilitating accelerated learning through personalized platforms that meet students' needs. Tools such as chatbots, virtual tutors and machine learning algorithms are being used to create adaptive and interactive learning experiences. This is particularly relevant to financial education, where the speed and effectiveness of learning can make a significant difference to the decisions people make about their money.

A notable example is the platform **Khan Academy**, which uses AI algorithms to personalize learning for each student. With a focus on personal finance and investing, Khan Academy offers courses that adjust to the student's progress, ensuring concepts are fully understood before moving on to more complex topics. This approach not only speeds up the learning process but also increases information retention.

Additionally, platforms like **Coursera** and **edX** are incorporating AI into their finance courses, allowing students to dynamically access relevant materials and resources. This personalization in education is not just a trend but a necessity in a world where information is available in abundance but is not always organized in a way that facilitates effective learning.

AI Tools for Smart Financial Decisions

With the help of AI, people are becoming more empowered to make informed financial decisions. Investment platforms like **Wealthfront** and **Betterment** utilize algorithms to provide personalized recommendations based on users' financial goals. These platforms not only help investors understand the markets, but also teach personal finance principles as users interact with them.

Additionally, financial management tools such as **As** and **YNAB (You Need A Budget)** are using AI to analyze spending habits and offer advice on how to save and invest more effectively. These apps help users visualize their finances in a way that wasn't previously possible, simplifying complex concepts and enabling more conscious money management.

By providing real-time insights and data analysis, AI allows users to not only learn but also apply that knowledge in practical ways. This type of dynamic and informative interaction is crucial for financial education, as users can see the immediate effects of their financial decisions and adjust their behavior accordingly.

Accessible Financial Education: Breaking Barriers

One of the biggest benefits of AI-based educational platforms is the democratization of access to financial knowledge. Through online courses, webinars and video tutorials, anyone with an internet connection can learn about personal finance and investing, regardless of their geographic location or economic status.

Initiatives like **Investopedia Academy** and **Smartly** are committed to making financial education accessible to everyone, offering courses that cover everything from the basics to advanced investing topics. AI plays a crucial role in this mission, facilitating the creation of content that meets the needs of different demographics and experience levels.

Additionally, platforms can collect data on users' learning preferences and behaviors, adjusting content according to audience demands. This means that instead of a fixed curriculum, students have access to materials that are relevant and up-to-date, thus increasing their chances of financial success.

Successful Examples: Millionaires Who Learned from AI

Many successful millionaires attribute their achievements to ongoing financial education and effective use of technology. **Dave Ramsey**, personal finance expert and best-selling author, uses digital platforms to share his philosophy on money and budgeting. It also promotes the use of financial apps that help users implement their strategies in a practical way.

Another example is **Ramit Sethi**, author of "I Will

Teach You to Be Rich", which combines financial education with digital marketing techniques to teach young people how to manage their money. Sethi uses AI to segment his audience and deliver content tailored to their needs, helping many change their mindset around finances.

These examples show how financial education, when combined with technology and AI, can empower individuals to transform their financial lives. The success stories of contemporary millionaires not only inspire, but also demonstrate that, with the right guidance and the right tools, anyone can achieve their financial goals.

The Future of Financial Education

As we move forward, the role of AI in financial education will continue to expand. Platforms that embrace emerging technologies will not only facilitate learning, but also create communities where individuals can share experiences and learn from each other. This collaboration will be vital to promoting a culture of financial education, where people feel empowered to make informed decisions about their money.

The future of financial education is being shaped by technological innovations and a user-centric approach, and AI is at the forefront of this transformation. With access to more effective and personalized educational resources, people are better equipped than ever to achieve wealth and financial success. By harnessing the power of AI, everyone can transform their financial potential and eventually embark on the path to financial freedom.

CHAPTER 7: THE IMPACT OF CRYPTOCURRENCIES AND BLOCKCHAIN

Introduction: The Financial Revolution of Cryptocurrencies

In recent years, cryptocurrencies and blockchain technology have made a transformative impact on the global financial landscape. Since the introduction of Bitcoin in 2009, these innovations have not only changed the way we think about money, but have also created new wealth opportunities for millions of people around the world. In this chapter, we'll explore how cryptocurrencies and blockchain are shaping the future of finance and how anyone can leverage these technologies to build their own fortune.

The rise of cryptocurrencies such as Bitcoin and Ethereum challenges the status quo of traditional financial systems. The decentralization offered by blockchain allows for faster, safer and more transparent transactions, removing intermediaries and reducing costs. This change not only benefits large investors, but also provides unique opportunities for ordinary individuals, allowing them to participate in a market that previously seemed inaccessible.

The Emergence of Cryptocurrencies:

A New Era of Investments

Cryptocurrencies emerged as a response to dissatisfaction with traditional financial systems, especially after the 2008 financial crisis. Bitcoin, the first cryptocurrency, was created with the aim of being a decentralized form of digital money. Since then, the cryptocurrency market has grown exponentially, giving rise to thousands of other coins and tokens.

Success stories involving cryptocurrencies are inspiring and illustrate the earning potential that this new market offers. For example, many investors who bought Bitcoin in its early years became millionaires when the price soared, going from a few cents to tens of thousands of dollars per unit. The case of **Erik Finman**, who invested $1,000 in Bitcoin when he was just 12 and became a millionaire at 18, is a notable example of the transformative potential of cryptocurrencies.

Ethereum and the World of NFTs: New Wealth Opportunities

In addition to Bitcoin, Ethereum revolutionized the market with its smart contracts platform, allowing the creation of decentralized applications and new types of digital assets, such as non-fungible tokens (NFTs). NFTs, which represent digital ownership of unique items such as art, music and collectibles, have opened up new avenues of investment and creativity.

The digital artist **Beeple** became a household name after selling a work of art as an NFT for a staggering $69 million at a Christie's auction. This event not only catapulted the visibility of NFTs but also inspired many to enter the space in search of similar opportunities. Today, anyone with a creative idea and a willingness to learn can explore creating and selling NFTs, participating in a booming market.

How to Invest in Cryptocurrencies: A Practical Guide

Entering the world of cryptocurrencies may seem intimidating, but there are several platforms and resources available that make the process easier for beginners. Exchanges like **Coinbase**, **Binance** and **Kraken** offer user-friendly interfaces that allow users to buy, sell and store cryptocurrencies with ease. Additionally, many educational resources are available, helping new investors better understand the market and the risks involved.

Investing in cryptocurrencies involves risks, and market volatility is an important factor to consider. However, with proper research and a solid strategy, investors can navigate this space effectively. A recommended approach is to diversify investments by allocating a portion of the portfolio to cryptocurrencies while maintaining a solid foundation in traditional assets such as stocks and bonds.

Blockchain and Its Role in Innovation

Blockchain technology is the backbone of cryptocurrencies, enabling a decentralized and secure system of record. However, its potential goes far beyond cryptocurrencies. Blockchain is being explored in several sectors, including healthcare, logistics and entertainment, to increase transparency and efficiency.

Companies like **IBM** and **Microsoft** are investing in blockchain-based solutions that promise to revolutionize the way information is managed and shared. This innovation not only presents opportunities for investors, but also for entrepreneurs who want to develop creative solutions to global problems. The emergence of startups using blockchain to improve traditional processes is a clear indication that demand for this technology will continue to grow.

The Future of Cryptocurrencies and Blockchain

As more people and companies adopt cryptocurrencies and blockchain technology, the future of these innovations looks promising. New regulations are being introduced, and the growing acceptance of cryptocurrencies as a legitimate form of payment is contributing to their legitimacy in the financial market. This creates a safer environment for investors and provides opportunities for growth.

For example, payment companies like **Square** and **PayPal** have already started allowing their users to buy, sell and use cryptocurrencies in their daily transactions. This demonstrates a growing acceptance of digital currency, and as more financial institutions adopt the technology, the trust and value of cryptocurrencies may continue to increase.

Opportunities for Everyone

The impact of cryptocurrencies and blockchain technology is redefining the concept of wealth and how people can achieve it. The stories of millionaires who invested in Bitcoin, Ethereum and NFTs are proof that, with courage and knowledge, anyone can enter this new world and create earning opportunities.

It's important to remember that while cryptocurrencies offer the potential for high returns, they also come with significant risks. Education and research are key for those looking to invest in this space. With the right tools and resources, the dream of becoming a millionaire through cryptocurrencies and blockchain is not just a possibility, but an achievable reality for everyone.

Thus, the key to wealth in the future may well lie in adopting these emerging technologies, making them an essential part of the million-dollar roadmap for everyone who aspires to financial success.

CHAPTER 8: AI IN THE INVESTMENT WORLD: HOW TO MAXIMIZE GAINS

Introduction to Artificial Intelligence in Investing

In recent years, Artificial Intelligence (AI) has emerged as a revolutionary tool in the investment world, allowing investors, both professional and amateur, to make more informed and efficient decisions. AI's ability to analyze large volumes of data in real time and identify hidden patterns is transforming the way portfolios are managed and investment strategies are developed.

Investors are increasingly turning to algorithms and AI-based platforms to gain insights that would previously have been impossible to discover manually. This chapter will explore the many ways in which AI is being used in the investment industry, from analyzing complex data to developing automated portfolios. Additionally, we will feature inspiring stories of millionaires who trusted AI to increase their profits and how this technology can be an ally on the path to riches.

Analyzing Complex Data with AI

Data analysis is one of the areas where AI really shines. The amount of data generated daily in the financial market is immense, and the ability to process and analyze this data quickly and accurately is crucial to the success of any investor. AI tools can quickly scan financial news, company reports and even social media data to identify sentiments and trends that could affect stock prices.

For example, the company **Sentifi** uses AI to analyze social media and news data, providing insights into public perception of different stocks and sectors. This allows investors to adjust their strategies based on real-time information, thus improving their chances of success.

Investing Robots: Automatic Portfolios

One of the most notable innovations at the intersection of AI and investing are robot investors, which automate portfolio management. These robots use advanced algorithms to allocate assets according to users' preferences and financial goals, minimizing risks and maximizing returns. Platforms like **Wealthfront** and **Betterment** have become popular for offering accessible, AI-based investment solutions.

Robo investors not only optimize asset allocation, but also rebalance portfolios automatically as market conditions change. This allows investors, especially those who do not have the experience or time to actively manage their investments, to still benefit from a solid investment strategy.

Examples of Millionaires and Success with AI

Success stories from investors who have used AI are inspiring and illustrate the potential of this technology. A notable example is that of **David Shaw**, founder of **D.E. Shaw Group**, one of the first firms to use AI algorithms for high-frequency trading. Shaw, a former computer science professor at Columbia, saw his hedge fund grow exponentially by employing data-driven strategies, establishing him as one of the most respected billionaires in the financial industry.

Another example is **Ray Dalio**, founder of **Bridgewater Associates**, which has adopted AI to complement its investment strategies. Dalio is known for his use of quantitative models and data analysis to identify market trends, resulting in consistent returns for his investors over the years.

These examples not only demonstrate the potential of AI, but also emphasize the importance of an adaptive and innovative mindset in the world of investing. As technology continues to evolve, those who embrace AI will be better positioned to thrive.

The Integration of AI in Investment Strategies

Integrating AI into investment strategies is not just limited to data analysis or the use of robot investors; it also involves creating predictive models that can help anticipate market movements. Machine learning-based models can identify correlations and patterns that may not be immediately evident to human analysts.

For example, the **Kensho**, a data analytics company, provides tools that allow investors to make informed predictions about how specific events may impact financial markets. This not only improves decision-making ability but also helps reduce the uncertainty associated with investing in volatile assets.

The Future of AI in Investments

As AI continues to develop, its role in the investment world will likely expand even further. Innovations like automating trading processes and customizing investment strategies based on user behavior are just some of the ways AI can continue to impact the industry.

The ability to generate real-time insights and optimize financial decisions will be within the reach of more and more investors, democratizing access to information that was previously exclusive to large financial institutions. With AI, the dream of becoming a millionaire is becoming more accessible than ever.

AI as an Ally on the Path to Wealth

Artificial Intelligence represents an unprecedented opportunity to maximize gains in the world of investments. By employing AI tools for data analysis, automated portfolio development, and predictive model creation, investors are better equipped to face the challenges of the modern market.

The examples of millionaires who trusted AI to increase their profits are an inspiration for everyone who aspires to financial success. The key to future success will be a willingness to embrace innovation and adapt to an ever-changing environment. As technology advances, the million map will become more accessible, and AI will be at the forefront of this transformation.

CHAPTER 9: MONETIZING SKILLS WITH DIGITAL PLATFORMS

The Digital Revolution and Modern Entrepreneurship

In recent years, the digital revolution has transformed the way people work, allowing ordinary individuals to monetize their skills in ways that were previously unimaginable. With the advancement of technology, especially Artificial Intelligence (AI), digital platforms like Fiverr, Upwork and YouTube have opened doors for freelancers and content creators around the world. In this chapter, we will explore how these platforms have allowed ordinary people to become millionaires by turning hobbies and talents into profitable businesses.

Digital platforms offer an accessible way for anyone to showcase their skills and services. Whether through selling graphic design, writing, programming, online classes or audiovisual content, the opportunities are endless. AI plays a crucial role in this scenario, facilitating the connection between service providers and customers, automating marketing processes and helping to optimize work. This chapter will delve deeper into how to maximize these opportunities.

Freelancing: The New Normal

Freelancing has become an attractive option for many, allowing flexibility and the possibility of unlimited earnings. Platforms like Upwork and Fiverr connect freelancers with clients in need of a variety of services. These platforms not only offer visibility but also provide tools and resources that help freelancers manage their businesses.

For example, freelancers can create detailed profiles that highlight their skills, experience, and work portfolios. This is particularly important in a competitive market where first impressions can make all the difference. Additionally, the platforms offer payment protection and customer support, which builds trust for both freelancers and clients.

Many successful freelancers started by offering their services for a low price to build a portfolio and receive positive reviews. After establishing a good reputation, they can increase their prices and attract higher-value customers. The key to success in freelancing is consistency and quality of work delivered.

Creating Content on YouTube:
From Passion to Profitability

YouTube has emerged as a powerful platform for monetizing skills and passions. Content creators can transform their experiences and knowledge into videos that attract a global audience. With the ability to generate income through advertisements, sponsorships and product sales, many have become millionaires in a matter of years.

A notable example is **MrBeast**, which started with videos of challenges and donations. He now generates millions in revenue and reinvests in his productions, creating a cycle of exponential growth. Another case is **Michelle Phan**, who became a beauty influencer and entrepreneur by monetizing her makeup tutorials.

To be successful on YouTube, it is essential to understand the platform's algorithm and how it rewards consistency and interaction with the audience. Creators who post regularly and engage with their followers are more likely to grow and monetize their channels.

Skills as Valuable Assets

What many people don't realize is that their skills can be considered valuable assets in the digital market. Skills in design, writing, programming, digital marketing and even hobbies like cooking or gardening can be monetized. Digital platforms make this possible by providing a space for individuals to offer their expertise and services.

For example, a person who has cooking skills might create a YouTube channel with recipes, sell recipe e-books, or offer online cooking classes. Likewise, someone who is good at graphic design can offer logo creation or digital marketing services on platforms like Fiverr.

AI can help with this process by providing insights into market trends, which allows service providers to adjust their offerings according to demand. Additionally, automation tools can help manage scheduling, marketing, and finances, allowing content creators to focus on their passions.

The Importance of Personal Branding

Building a personal brand is essential in the digital world. How freelancers and content creators present themselves can make a big difference in their ability to attract clients and audiences. Personal branding involves not only visual design, but also communication and authenticity.

Having an attractive profile on freelancing platforms, a well-designed YouTube channel, and an active social media presence are crucial components of personal branding. This online presence helps establish credibility and trust, key factors in converting visitors into paying customers.

Successful freelancers invest time in creating content that resonates with their target audience and reflects their personality and values. This not only helps you attract customers, but also maintain a loyal audience that can translate into recurring sales.

Success Stories: Turning Hobbies into Wealth

The world is full of inspiring stories of people who turned hobbies into profitable ventures. For example, **Pat Flynn** started his blog "Smart Passive Income" as a side project, sharing tips on how to generate income online. Not only has he built a loyal following, but he has also become a best-selling author and an influencer in the field of digital marketing.

Another example is **Katherine Johnson**, who started sharing her cake recipes on Instagram. Her love for baking quickly turned into a successful business, where she now sells online courses and related products. These examples illustrate how it is possible to monetize passions and skills, achieving financial freedom.

Future of Work: The Evolution of Digital Opportunities

As the digital world continues to evolve, monetization opportunities will also grow. With the rise of AI, new platforms and tools are expected to emerge, making the process of transforming skills into profit even easier. User experience personalization and process automation will make it easier for freelancers and content creators to manage their activities and maximize their earnings.

The "work from anywhere" trend is also expected to continue, allowing individuals from around the world to access the global marketplace. Remote work is not just a convenience; It's an opportunity to expand horizons and reach a wider audience.

Monetizing What You Love

The ability to monetize skills through digital platforms is a revolution that has democratized entrepreneurship. With the support of AI and digital tools, anyone can become a successful freelancer or content creator. The secret is to identify your passions, invest in developing skills and have an action plan.

For those willing to learn and adapt, the sky is the limit. The path to becoming a millionaire can start with one simple step: turning your skills and passions into a business. The digital age offers the tools; It's up to you to take advantage of the opportunities that arise.

CHAPTER 10: THE POWER OF AUTOMATION IN E-COMMERCE

The E-commerce Revolution

In recent years, e-commerce has transformed into one of the most dynamic sectors of the global economy, driven by technological innovation and growing consumer acceptance of online shopping. One of the biggest innovations in this space is automation, which allows entrepreneurs to create profitable online stores without the traditional complications of inventory management or customer service. With the help of Artificial Intelligence (AI), automation is reshaping the way businesses operate, making e-commerce more accessible and efficient than ever.

Automation in e-commerce involves the implementation of technologies that allow repetitive tasks to be performed with minimal human intervention. This can include everything from inventory management to personalizing the customer experience. With automated tools, entrepreneurs can focus on growth and innovation strategies rather than getting lost in administrative tasks.

Inventory Management: Automation as a Solution

Inventory management is one of the most

challenging areas for e-commerce companies, especially for those that don't want to deal with physically storing products. Automation allows businesses to utilize inventory management systems that automatically monitor product availability, orders, and replenishments.

These AI-based systems can predict demand based on historical data and market trends, adjusting inventory levels in real time. For example, platforms like Shopify and WooCommerce offer automation solutions that allow stores to monitor inventory levels without manual intervention. This reduces the risk of excess stock or product shortages, resulting in efficiency and cost savings.

Furthermore, with the use of integration technologies, companies can automate the connection between their inventory systems and their sales channels, ensuring that information is always up to date. This level of automation not only improves the customer experience, but also frees up store owners to focus on more strategic areas of their business.

Automated Marketing Campaigns

Another area where automation has a significant impact is in marketing campaigns. With marketing automation tools, business owners can segment their audiences more effectively and personalize their communications. Platforms like Mailchimp and HubSpot allow companies to create automated email campaigns that adapt to consumer behavior.

These platforms use AI algorithms to analyze customer data and predict which products or promotions might be most appealing. For example, if a customer viewed a product, the company could send an automated email offering a discount on that specific item. This not only increases conversion rates but also improves the customer experience by making communication more relevant and personalized.

In addition to email campaigns, automation also allows companies to manage their social media more effectively. Tools like Hootsuite and Buffer allow you to schedule posts and monitor engagement, freeing up precious time for business owners to focus on creating quality content and engaging with their customers.

Automated Customer Service

Customer service is one of the areas where automation can have a profound impact. AI-powered chatbots and virtual assistants are becoming increasingly common in e-commerce, enabling businesses to provide 24/7 support. These bots can answer frequently asked questions, solve simple problems, and even process orders, all without the need for human intervention.

Companies like Zappos and Sephora have already implemented chatbots to help customers with their questions and concerns. These systems not only improve the customer experience, but also save resources by allowing employees to focus on more complex issues that require a human touch.

Automation in customer service also enables more effective data collection. With interactions being recorded, companies can analyze trends and customer feedback, enabling continuous improvements to their products and services. This creates a virtuous feedback loop that is beneficial to both the company and the customer.

Successful Examples: Entrepreneurs Who Used Automation

Many entrepreneurs are reaping the benefits of automation in e-commerce and transforming their ideas into successful businesses. For example, **Oberlo** is a platform that allows entrepreneurs to do dropshipping, eliminating the need to manage inventory. With automation, business owners can easily import products from suppliers, automate orders, and manage sales, all with one click.

Another example is the **TeeSpring**, which allows content creators to design and sell custom t-shirts without worrying about managing inventory or production. Automation allows them to focus on marketing and creating new designs, while the platform takes care of the rest.

These examples demonstrate how automation can turn a simple idea into a thriving business. As more people recognize the advantages of operating automated online stores, e-commerce is likely to continue to grow exponentially.

Future of E-commerce: The Rise of Automation

The future of e-commerce looks increasingly automated. As AI and machine learning technologies advance, we can expect companies to be able to predict customer needs even more accurately and offer more personalized shopping experiences.

Automation is not just limited to inventory management and marketing; it can also include personalization of the user experience in real time. As systems become more sophisticated, it will be possible to adapt the user interface, recommended products and special offers based on individual customer preferences, making the shopping experience more intuitive and enjoyable.

Additionally, new technologies such as augmented and virtual reality are starting to enter the e-commerce space, offering customers the opportunity to try products before purchasing them. Automation will be key to integrating these technologies and ensuring the customer experience remains fluid and engaging.

The Impact of Automation on E-commerce

Automation in e-commerce is not just a passing

trend; it is a fundamental change in the way businesses operate. It allows entrepreneurs to create profitable online stores without the hassle of dealing with inventory or customer service. The combination of automated tools and AI is revolutionizing inventory management, marketing campaigns and customer service, providing a more efficient experience for both business owners and consumers.

As e-commerce continues to grow and develop, automation will be a central element in creating sustainable and profitable business models. For entrepreneurs who are ready to take advantage of these tools, the future is bright, with the promise of new opportunities and exponential growth. The age of automation has just begun, and those who adapt quickly will reap the rewards of this digital revolution.

CHAPTER 11: SMART INVESTING WITH AI

The New Investment Paradigm

The digital transformation that has been occurring in several industries has also significantly impacted the financial sector, especially the field of investments. Artificial Intelligence (AI) is at the heart of this revolution, enabling more sophisticated and personalized approaches to portfolio construction. Previously restricted to institutional investors and hedge funds, AI tools are now accessible to any investor, democratizing access to knowledge and investment strategies.

AI allows for large-scale data analysis, making it easier to identify patterns that would be impossible to detect using traditional methods. Machines can process immense amounts of information in seconds, from financial reports and market data to news and social media. This not only improves forecast accuracy but also allows investors to adjust their strategies in real time.

Risk and Return Analysis

One of the main benefits of AI in investing is its ability to create personalized portfolios based on risk analysis and market projections. Through complex algorithms, AI systems can assess an investor's risk appetite by analyzing factors such as age, financial situation, investment objectives and risk tolerance. With this information, AI can suggest the ideal asset allocation, balancing investments across stocks, bonds, real estate, and other asset classes.

For example, platforms like Wealthfront and Betterment use algorithms to offer automated investment advice. These systems constantly analyze asset performance and adjust allocations based on changing market conditions, helping investors maximize their returns while minimizing risk.

Additionally, AI can identify correlations between different assets that may not be evident to the average investor. This allows portfolio diversification to be more efficient, reducing volatility and increasing return potential. Studies show that diversification is one of the most important factors for long-term investment success, and AI facilitates this practice in innovative ways.

AI Market Forecasts

AI's ability to analyze large volumes of data in real time allows it to make more accurate market predictions. Predictive models can identify emerging trends and signs of changing economic conditions before they become evident to the broader market. This gives investors a competitive advantage by allowing them to adjust their strategies before market swings materialize.

For example, AI systems like the one used by BlackRock, one of the world's largest asset managers, analyze real-time market data to predict price movements and identify investment opportunities. These systems are capable of processing information from different sources, including economic, financial and social data, to provide valuable insights into the future.

With AI, investors can benefit from a more data-driven approach, minimizing impulsive decisions that often result in financial losses. Instead of relying on intuitions or speculation, investors can now make decisions based on objective analysis, increasing the chances of success in their investments.

Dynamic Portfolios and Automatic Rebalancing

Another crucial aspect of using AI in investing is the ability to create dynamic portfolios that automatically adjust to market conditions. Automatic rebalancing allows investors to maintain their desired asset allocation without the need for constant manual intervention. This is particularly useful in a volatile market environment where conditions can change quickly.

Platforms using AI can continuously monitor asset performance and adjust allocations in real time, ensuring the portfolio remains aligned with the investor's objectives. This automation not only saves time but also minimizes the risk of emotional decisions that can compromise portfolio performance.

Furthermore, AI can integrate different investment strategies, such as value investing and growth investing, into a single portfolio. This allows investors to benefit from multiple approaches and quickly adapt to changing market conditions, enhancing their chances of success.

Opportunities for All Investors

The democratization of access to AI tools is enabling investors of all levels to benefit from advanced investment strategies. Previously, only institutional and high-net-worth investors had access to these technologies, but now, with the emergence of platforms like Robinhood, Acorns, and M1 Finance, anyone can start investing with the help of AI.

These platforms offer analysis and portfolio management capabilities that were previously only available to financial professionals. This not only empowers individual investors, but also helps foster a culture of financial literacy, where investors are more informed and empowered to make decisions.

Additionally, AI can help investors identify opportunities in emerging markets and innovative sectors that may not receive due attention. For example, investments in sustainable technologies and biotechnology companies are growing rapidly, and AI can help identify the best options within these sectors, boosting portfolio growth.

Ethical Considerations and Risks of AI in Investments

Despite the many benefits of AI in the investment landscape, there are also ethical considerations and risks that need to be taken into account. Overreliance on algorithms can lead to investment decisions that fail to consider important human and social factors. Additionally, transparency in AI platforms' decision-making processes is critical to ensuring investors understand how their decisions are being made.

Cybersecurity issues are also a growing concern. As more investors adopt digital platforms to manage their investments, protection against fraud and cyberattacks becomes essential. Companies must ensure that their security measures are robust and that investor data is protected.

The Future of AI Investing

The future of AI investing looks promising as technologies continue to evolve. We can expect an increase in the personalization of investment strategies, with tools that further adapt to individual investor needs. Furthermore, AI will play a key role in identifying new asset classes and analyzing alternative investments such as cryptocurrencies and tokenized assets.

Innovations in AI can also lead to greater integration between different markets and sectors, allowing investors to more easily explore global opportunities. With the continued evolution of AI technologies, the investment landscape will become increasingly accessible and diverse.

Building Wealth with AI

In short, Artificial Intelligence is transforming the investment landscape, allowing the creation of personalized portfolios and facilitating risk and return analysis. With democratized access to these technologies, any investor can take advantage of automation and data-driven analytics to build wealth quickly.

As AI continues to evolve, its influence on investing will only increase, providing new opportunities for all investors. The key to success will be staying informed about technological innovations and adopting an open mindset to the new possibilities that AI can bring to the world of investing.

CHAPTER 12: AI TOOLS FOR BUDDING ENTREPRENEURS

The Current Scenario for Entrepreneurs

In the contemporary business environment, Artificial Intelligence (AI) tools have become indispensable for small entrepreneurs looking to optimize their operations, increase efficiency and drive growth. AI technology allows even the most modest businesses to access capabilities previously only available to large companies, democratizing access to innovative solutions. This is crucial in a world where agility and adaptability are key to success.

The use of AI tools not only facilitates the automation of routine tasks, but also provides valuable insights through data analysis, helping entrepreneurs make informed decisions. In this chapter, we'll explore some of the top AI tools accessible to small business owners, including customer relationship management (CRM) systems, marketing automation platforms, and data analytics tools.

Smart CRMs: Transforming Customer Relationships

Customer relationship management (CRM) systems are fundamental to the growth of any business, allowing entrepreneurs to manage their interactions with customers and potential customers efficiently. Smart CRM solutions like Salesforce, HubSpot, and Zoho CRM use AI to optimize lead management and automate follow-up, allowing entrepreneurs to focus on closing deals and building lasting relationships.

These smart CRMs offer advanced features like predictive analytics that help you identify which leads are most likely to convert. This is done through the analysis of historical and behavioral data, allowing entrepreneurs to prioritize their sales efforts more effectively. Additionally, automating routine tasks like sending follow-up emails and scheduling meetings frees up valuable time for entrepreneurs to focus on strategic activities.

Another important feature of modern CRMs is integration with other business tools, such as digital marketing platforms and accounting systems. This integration allows for a holistic view of the business, facilitating data collection and collaboration between different departments. With these tools, entrepreneurs can not only improve their sales, but also offer a more personalized and satisfying experience for customers.

Marketing Automation Platforms: Accelerating Growth

Marketing automation is another area where AI tools can have a significant impact on small business growth. Platforms like Mailchimp, ActiveCampaign, and Marketo offer robust solutions that allow entrepreneurs to create and manage marketing campaigns effectively, saving time and resources.

These platforms use AI algorithms to segment audiences, personalize content, and optimize campaigns based on real-time performance data. For example, customer segmentation allows entrepreneurs to send more relevant and targeted messages, increasing open and conversion rates. Additionally, automating the sending of emails and social media posts ensures that content is delivered at the right time, maximizing engagement.

Data analytics also plays a crucial role in marketing automation platforms. Entrepreneurs can monitor the performance of their campaigns, evaluate which tactics are working, and adjust their strategies based on hard data. With detailed reporting and actionable insights, entrepreneurs can make informed decisions about where to invest their marketing resources to get the highest return on investment.

Data Analysis Tools: Making Informed Decisions

Data analysis tools such as Google Analytics, Tableau and Microsoft Power BI are essential for helping entrepreneurs understand their business performance and make data-driven decisions. These platforms allow entrepreneurs to collect, analyze and visualize data from multiple sources, making it easier to identify trends and opportunities.

With the help of AI, these tools can automate the analysis of large volumes of data, extracting insights that would be difficult to identify manually. For example, entrepreneurs can use predictive analytics to anticipate customer behavior, adjusting their marketing and sales strategies based on the predictions. This not only improves efficiency but also increases the chances of success.

Furthermore, data visualization is an important part of the analysis process. Tools like Tableau allow entrepreneurs to create interactive dashboards that present information in a clear and accessible way. This is crucial for communicating results and strategies to teams and investors, facilitating collaboration and alignment around common goals.

The Future with AI Tools

As technology advances, the role of AI tools in the lives of budding entrepreneurs will continue to grow. Process automation, customer service personalization, and real-time data analysis are just a few of the ways AI can help drive business growth. For small entrepreneurs, adopting these tools is not just a competitive advantage; It is a necessity to survive and thrive in an increasingly challenging business environment.

In a world where speed and efficiency are key, AI tools have become essential allies for entrepreneurs who want to not just keep up, but lead. With access to these innovative technologies, anyone can turn their entrepreneurial vision into reality, propelling their business towards success.

CHAPTER 13: THE GIG ECONOMY AND THE NEW WEALTH

The Rise of the Gig Economy

In recent years, the gig economy — or temporary work economy — has emerged as a global phenomenon, driven by the growth of digital platforms. This work model, which involves freelancers and independent workers, allows individuals to complete tasks and projects rather than committing to a traditional full-time job. This transition has revolutionized the way people earn money, creating new opportunities for wealth for those willing to explore this new way of working.

The advent of apps and platforms like Uber, Airbnb, Fiverr and Upwork has made it easier for service providers and consumers to connect. This unprecedented market access has allowed people of different backgrounds and skills to monetize their talents and resources. The gig economy not only offers flexibility, but also democratizes the ability to generate income, allowing anyone to become a potential entrepreneur.

A fundamental aspect of the gig economy is its resilience in times of economic crisis. During the COVID-19 pandemic, many workers have faced layoffs and cut hours. In response, many have turned to the gig economy to support their finances. This not only demonstrated the adaptability of this working model, but also how it can become a viable source of income in challenging times.

The Impact of Technology and AI

Emerging technologies, especially Artificial Intelligence (AI), play a key role in optimizing activities in the gig economy. Digital platforms are increasingly using AI algorithms to match workers with opportunities that match their skills and preferences. This not only improves efficiency, but also allows freelancers to optimize their proposals and improve their chances of success.

For example, transportation apps like Uber and Lyft use AI to determine the best routes and estimate arrival times, while delivery platforms like DoorDash and Postmates use algorithms to optimize deliveries and maximize drivers' earnings. Likewise, freelancing sites use AI tools to analyze freelancers' performance, offering insights that help improve work quality and increase visibility.

Additionally, AI can be used to automate administrative tasks such as scheduling and invoicing, allowing freelancers to focus on what they do best: providing services. This is especially beneficial for those managing multiple projects simultaneously, a common feature in the gig economy. The result is greater efficiency and the potential to increase income.

Gig Economy Success Stories

Many individuals have excelled in the gig economy, turning their skills into lucrative careers. A notable example is the case of Julie B. (not her real name), a graphic designer who started offering her services on Fiverr. Initially, she charged low prices to attract clients and build a portfolio. Over time, her reputation grew, and she was able to increase her rates, eventually becoming one of the top sellers on the platform. Today, Julie generates six-figure annual income, demonstrating how the gig economy can turn talent into wealth.

Another inspiring example is a wedding photographer who used platforms like Instagram and Pinterest to promote his work. By building a personal brand and engaging with his audience, he was able to not only find clients, but also create digital products such as photography guides and online courses. This income diversification exemplifies how the gig economy allows individuals to explore multiple sources of income, increasing their chances of financial success.

These stories are just the tip of the iceberg. The gig economy is full of individuals who, through creativity and hard work, have managed to change their financial lives. The accessibility and flexibility of this work model attract more and more people, driving social and economic transformation.

The Future of Gig Economy and AI

As the gig economy continues to grow, the integration of AI into digital platforms will deepen. Automation and data analysis are expected to become even more sophisticated, allowing freelancers to maximize their earning potential. With increasingly accessible AI tools, independent workers will be able to make more informed decisions about which projects to take on, what skills to develop, and how to manage their time more efficiently.

Furthermore, the trend of platforms specializing in specific niches is expanding. While platforms like Upwork serve a wide range of services, new platforms are emerging to connect freelancers in specialized fields like digital art, technical writing, and consulting. This creates additional opportunities for those looking to excel in specific areas and build a more loyal customer base.

The gig economy, supported by digital platforms and AI technology, is transforming the way people work and generate income. The opportunities for extraordinary gains are real and available to anyone willing to explore this new paradigm. With inspiring success stories and an environment that fosters innovation and flexibility, the gig economy represents not only a shift in traditional employment but also a viable route to building wealth.

As technology continues to evolve and the global economy adapts, the possibilities for independent workers and freelancers will only increase. The future of the gig economy is bright, and those who embrace this change will be well positioned to reap the rewards of this new era of wealth.

CHAPTER 14: TECH ENTREPRENEURSHIP: THE NEXT FRONTIER

The Rise of Tech Entrepreneurship

In recent years, technological entrepreneurship has emerged as one of the most dynamic and innovative segments of the global economy. Driven by the evolution of Artificial Intelligence (AI) and blockchain technology, entrepreneurs are developing solutions that not only meet emerging needs, but also create new business opportunities. This chapter explores how this new frontier is shaping the future of work and wealth, enabling ordinary individuals to become millionaires.

The exponential growth of AI and blockchain is not just a passing trend; represents a revolution in the way business is conducted. Startups using these technologies are transforming entire industries, from finance to healthcare, education and logistics. For example, AI is being used to develop more efficient customer service systems, while blockchain offers security and transparency solutions that are revolutionizing financial transactions.

With increasing digitalization, more entrepreneurs are realizing the opportunities created by these technologies. The barrier to entry for technology entrepreneurship is lowering, allowing people with diverse knowledge, not just those with a technical background, to enter the field. This democratization of access is creating an ecosystem where innovation can thrive, regardless of where entrepreneurs come from.

The Role of AI and Blockchain in Entrepreneurship

AI is transforming entrepreneurship by automating processes, optimizing operations and improving decision making. Predictive analytics tools, for example, help business owners better understand consumer behavior, allowing them to customize products and services to meet the needs of their target audience. This not only increases customer satisfaction, but also boosts sales, creating a sustainable growth cycle.

On the other hand, blockchain is redefining the way companies manage their operations. By offering a decentralized and secure system for recording transactions, blockchain eliminates the need for intermediaries, reducing costs and increasing efficiency. This is especially relevant in sectors such as finance and logistics, where transparency and security are crucial.

Entrepreneurs who adopt these technologies have the chance to stand out in a competitive market. One notable example is the growth of startups offering blockchain-based solutions for supply chain tracking, allowing companies to prove the authenticity and origin of their products. This not only improves consumer confidence but also generates significant value for brands.

Stories of Millionaires in Technological Entrepreneurship

Many entrepreneurs stood out in this new scenario, building empires based on innovative technological solutions. One example is the story of Vitalik Buterin, co-founder of Ethereum, a blockchain-based platform that enabled the development of smart contracts. His vision of a decentralized internet has not only spawned a new wave of startups, but also made him one of the most influential young billionaires in the world.

Another example is the trajectory of companies like Airbnb and Uber, which, although not exclusively based on AI or blockchain, use emerging technologies to disrupt traditional sectors. The ability of these entrepreneurs to rapidly scale their businesses and create new service-based economies is a testament to the potential of technology entrepreneurship.

These inspiring stories show that entry into technological entrepreneurship is not restricted to programmers or engineers. Increasingly, people with varied backgrounds are coming together to form diverse teams, bringing different perspectives and experiences to the development of innovative solutions.

How to Enter the Technological Entrepreneurship Market

For those who want to venture into the world of technology entrepreneurship, opportunities are abundant. One of the keys to success is identifying a problem to be solved. This can be done through market research and customer feedback, allowing entrepreneurs to develop products and services that truly meet the needs of the public.

Furthermore, it is essential to build a network of contacts. Attending technology events, conferences and meetups is an excellent way to meet other entrepreneurs and investors. Networking can open doors to partnerships, investments and growth opportunities.

Finally, ongoing education is essential. With the rapid pace of technological change, staying up to date on industry trends and learning new skills are crucial to standing out.

Online courses, workshops and mentoring can provide the knowledge needed to navigate this constantly evolving field.

The Future of Technological Entrepreneurship

The future of technological entrepreneurship is promising and full of possibilities. With the growing adoption of AI and blockchain, new business opportunities will continue to emerge, and innovation will be the engine that drives this evolution. As more people enter this market, the diversity of ideas and solutions will expand, creating a fertile environment for economic growth.

Furthermore, technology entrepreneurship is expected to play a crucial role in solving global problems such as climate change, social inequality and public health. By developing technology-based solutions, entrepreneurs have the opportunity to not only create wealth, but also generate a positive impact on society.

The ability for anyone to become a technological entrepreneur, regardless of their training or experience, is one of the greatest promises of this new era. With creativity, determination and the right tools, anyone can explore this new frontier and potentially become a millionaire in the process.

17 HOW AI IS REVOLUTIONIZING DIGITAL MARKETING

1. DATA ANALYSIS AND BEHAVIOR PREDICTION

One of the biggest benefits of AI in digital marketing is its ability to analyze large volumes of data in real time. AI tools allow companies to gain detailed insights into consumer behavior by precisely segmenting audiences.

For example, machine learning algorithms can predict consumers' purchasing patterns, suggesting which products or services they are most likely to purchase. Amazon, for example, uses AI to suggest products based on a user's purchasing history and browsing behavior, increasing its conversion and engagement rates.

These analyzes help companies adapt their marketing messages much more efficiently. Instead of generic campaigns, ads are precisely targeted to target audiences, resulting in more effective campaigns and greater return on investment (ROI).

2. PERSONALIZATION AT SCALE

Personalization is one of the most valuable aspects of AI in digital marketing. Platforms that use AI can create personalized marketing campaigns for each user based on their behavior, preferences and past interactions. With the power of AI, this personalization can be done on a scale that would be impossible manually.

Companies like Netflix and Spotify use AI to personalize content recommendations for their users. In digital marketing, AI can be used to personalize emails, ads, and even landing pages to ensure each user sees the content most relevant to them. This personalization not only improves user experience but also increases conversion rates.

3. REAL-TIME CAMPAIGN OPTIMIZATION

Another big advantage of AI in digital marketing is its ability to optimize campaigns in real time. Previously, marketers had to wait for a campaign to end to analyze the results and make adjustments. With AI, this has changed.

Today, AI algorithms can automatically adjust campaigns based on performance. If an ad isn't generating the expected clicks, AI can modify the copy, adjust the target audience, or change the budget to improve results. This ability to automatically adjust ensures that campaigns are always optimized to achieve the best possible performance.

4. CHATBOTS AND AUTOMATED CUSTOMER SERVICE

AI is also revolutionizing customer service, an essential aspect of digital marketing. Intelligent chatbots, such as companies like Sephora and Domino's Pizza, allow interactions with consumers 24 hours a day, seven days a week. These chatbots are programmed to answer frequently asked questions, provide product recommendations, and even process orders.

In addition to improving the customer experience, chatbots help companies save time and resources. This is especially important for small businesses that may not have the resources to maintain a large customer service team.

5. PROGRAMMATIC ADS WITH AI

Programmatic advertising, powered by AI, is changing the way digital ads are bought and sold. Programmatic advertising uses AI to automate online ad buying, which allows businesses to reach more specific audiences more effectively.

Companies like Google and Facebook use AI to deliver personalized ads based on a user's interests, behavior and location. This not only increases the relevance of ads but also significantly improves the ROI of marketing campaigns.

6. THE IMPORTANCE OF SMART SEO

AI is also transforming SEO (Search Engine Optimization), one of the main digital marketing strategies. AI tools can analyze web content and suggest improvements so that pages rank better in search engines.

For example, the SEO platform "MarketMuse" uses AI to analyze content pages and suggest topics that are missing to make them more robust and relevant for Google's algorithms. This helps businesses improve their online visibility and consequently attract more organic traffic.

EXAMPLES OF SUCCESS WITH AI IN DIGITAL MARKETING

Several highly successful entrepreneurs and companies are using AI to boost their digital marketing campaigns and build business empires.

1. **Coca-cola**: Coca-Cola uses AI to analyze social media data and customer feedback, which helps it adjust its advertising campaigns in real time. In 2017, Coca-Cola launched its first fully AI-designed advertising campaign, based on consumer-generated data.
2. **Nike**: Nike uses AI to create personalized shopping experiences for its customers. Through its app, the company recommends products based on the user's purchasing behavior and preferences. Additionally, Nike uses AI to create dynamic ads that automatically change based on consumer interests and actions.
3. **Airbnb**: Airbnb uses AI to optimize its prices and predict demand for accommodation in different locations. Additionally, the company uses AI to improve the user experience by offering personalized accommodation and destination recommendations.

AI AS THE FUTURE OF DIGITAL MARKETING

The AI-powered digital marketing revolution is just beginning. As technology advances, we will see even more innovations that will enable increasingly effective and personalized campaigns. Entrepreneurs who use AI to optimize their marketing strategies are ahead of the curve, creating empires and achieving previously unimaginable levels of success.

The future of digital marketing will be largely dominated by intelligent algorithms that will continue to refine and improve the way companies reach their consumers. The use of AI is not just a competitive advantage — it is quickly becoming a necessity for any company that wants to thrive in the digital economy.

Companies and entrepreneurs that embrace this technology are now reaping the rewards, while those who resist adopting it may be left behind.

CHAPTER 16: INVESTING IN TECHNOLOGICAL INNOVATIONS

The Revolution of Technological Innovations

In the 21st century, investing in technological innovations, especially in areas such as Artificial Intelligence (AI) and technological startups, is becoming one of the most attractive strategies for those seeking to build fortunes. Technology is developing at an unprecedented rate, creating fertile ground for investments that can generate substantial returns. For investors, understanding how to identify emerging trends and capitalize on these opportunities can be the key to financial success.

With increasing digitalization, AI is at the forefront of this technological revolution. According to McKinsey, the potential impact of AI on the global economy could reach trillions of dollars in the coming years. This represents not only an opportunity for companies developing AI-based solutions, but also a chance for investors who know how to identify which startups are ahead of the curve.

Identifying Emerging Trends

Identifying emerging trends is essential for any investor who wants to enter the world of technological innovations. The first step in this process is to understand the current market scenario. The increasing use of AI in industries as diverse as healthcare, finance, transportation and marketing offers valuable clues about where the next big opportunities may emerge. For example, process automation and predictive analytics are changing the way companies operate, and investors who recognize these patterns can benefit significantly.

Another approach is to watch for changes in government regulations and policies that may impact specific industries. The growing emphasis on data privacy and cybersecurity, for example, has created a demand for technology solutions that ensure regulatory compliance. Startups that offer technologies to protect data or that focus on privacy solutions can represent promising investment opportunities.

Crowdfunding and collective investment platforms have also become a valuable tool for investors looking to engage with early-stage startups. These platforms allow individual investors to fund projects and ideas that resonate with their visions, creating an ecosystem where innovations can thrive. By doing so, investors can participate in the growth of technologies that have the potential to transform entire industries.

Examples of Successful Investments

Several investors have achieved great returns by investing in technological innovations. An example is **Peter Thiel**, co-founder of PayPal and an early investor in Facebook. His ability to identify Facebook's potential before it became a technology giant has made him billions. Thiel is known for his focus on companies that challenge the status quo and that have the potential to grow exponentially.

Another example is **Marc Andreessen**, co-founder of Netscape and venture capital investor who co-founded

Andreessen Horowitz. The company has invested in several successful startups, including Twitter and Airbnb, that have transformed their industries. Andreessen Horowitz's strategy of focusing on companies that are at the forefront of innovation has helped it create a robust and diversified portfolio, resulting in substantial returns for its investors.

The Role of Investment Funds and Venture Capital

Investment funds and venture capital firms play a crucial role in identifying and financing technological innovations. They not only offer capital but also provide guidance and strategic support to startups. Institutional investors have the ability to analyze market trends on a large scale, allowing them to identify opportunities that may go unnoticed by individual investors.

Increasing competition between venture capital funds also means that innovative startups have more funding options than ever before. This creates an environment conducive to innovation, where new ideas can be tested and developed quickly. For investors, this means they can access a constant stream of opportunities to invest in emerging technologies.

The Importance of Diversification

Investing in technological innovations, especially in startups, involves risks. Many startups fail, and the capital invested can be lost. Therefore, diversification is essential. Investors should consider creating a portfolio that includes a variety of startups in different stages of development and sectors. This approach helps mitigate risks and increase the chances of positive returns.

Another way to diversify is to invest in venture capital funds or ETFs (exchange-traded funds) that focus on technology. These instruments allow investors to have exposure to a variety of companies rather than relying on a single startup. Diversification not only protects against losses, but also opens doors to opportunities that may not be accessible otherwise.

The Future of Technological Innovations

As we move forward, the future of technological innovations looks promising. New technologies such as blockchain, the Internet of Things (IoT) and biotechnology are becoming increasingly integrated into the global economy. For investors, this means that investment opportunities will continue to grow as more industries adopt these technologies.

Furthermore, the increasing focus on sustainability and eco-friendly solutions is creating a new field of investment. Startups that tackle environmental problems like climate change and pollution are attracting attention and funding. This not only provides opportunities for financial returns, but also allows investors to contribute to a more sustainable future.

In short, investing in technological innovations and AI startups offers an exciting and potentially lucrative path to building fortunes. By identifying emerging trends, diversifying investments and tracking market changes, investors can position themselves to capitalize on the opportunities the future holds. The key is to stay informed, open to new ideas, and willing to act when opportunities present themselves.

CHAPTER 17: EXPERIENCE ECONOMY AND PERSONALIZATION WITH AI

The Emergence of the Experience Economy

In recent years, the experience economy has emerged as a new economic paradigm, where consumers are increasingly willing to pay more for personalized experiences and products. This phenomenon is driven by the growing demand for unique and memorable interactions rather than simple commercial transactions. According to a report from *Harvard Business Review*, companies that prioritize customer experience not only excel in their respective industries, but also achieve faster, more sustainable growth. This shift in focus to experience and personalization offers significant opportunities for companies that can integrate Artificial Intelligence (AI) into their strategies.

AI plays a crucial role in personalization, enabling companies to analyze large-scale data to better understand consumer behavior and preferences. With this, they can create more relevant and personalized offers, increasing customer satisfaction and brand loyalty. This approach not only improves the consumer experience, but also boosts sales, as satisfied consumers are more likely to recommend products and services to others.

Personalization as a Competitive Differentiator

Personalization has become a competitive differentiator in a saturated market. Companies like Amazon and Netflix are clear examples of how AI-based personalization can transform the customer experience. Amazon, for example, uses recommendation algorithms that analyze users' purchasing behavior, suggesting products that align with their preferences. This not only improves the shopping experience but also increases the likelihood of repeat purchases.

Similarly, Netflix uses viewing data to offer personalized movie and series recommendations. This strategy not only improves subscriber retention but also increases viewing time on the platform. Studies show that personalized recommendations can increase a user's likelihood of watching new content by up to 80%. This highlights the importance of personalization and how it can be applied across industries.

The Role of AI in Creating Personalized Experiences

AI not only facilitates personalization but also enables the creation of unique experiences. For example, in the tourism industry, companies are using AI-based chatbots to provide personalized travel recommendations. These chatbots can interact with customers in real time, analyzing their preferences and travel history to offer relevant suggestions. Additionally, AI can help predict behavior patterns, allowing companies to anticipate consumer needs.

An interesting example is the use of AI in live events and experiences. Some companies are using facial recognition technology to personalize event experiences, offering relevant content based on attendees' preferences. This approach not only enriches the customer experience, but also allows companies to collect valuable data on audience behavior.

The Value of Personalization in the Customer Experience

Personalization generates significant value in the customer experience. Consumers are willing to pay more for products and services that meet their individual needs. A study carried out by *PwC* revealed that 86% of consumers are willing to pay more for a personalized customer service experience. This demonstrates that by investing in personalization strategies, companies not only improve the customer experience but can also increase their profit margin.

Additionally, personalization can result in an increase in customer loyalty. Consumers who feel valued and understood are more likely to return and make repeat purchases. This creates a positive cycle where personalization leads to a better customer experience, which in turn results in greater loyalty and, ultimately, an increase in sales.

Success Stories in AI and Personalization Implementation

Several companies are excelling in implementing AI for personalization and experience savings. Sephora, for example, uses AI technology to offer personalized product recommendations based on customer preferences. Furthermore, its application of a virtual assistant helps consumers find the right products according to their specific needs. This approach not only improves the shopping experience but also results in a significant increase in sales.

Another example is Nike, which created a personalization platform that allows consumers to customize their own products. Nike By You allows users to choose colors, materials and styles, creating a unique product that reflects their preferences. This not only increases customer engagement but also generates a memorable experience that encourages brand loyalty.

The Future of the Experience and Personalization Economy

The future of the experience economy and AI-powered personalization is promising. As technology advances, opportunities for customization expand. Companies that invest in AI and personalized solutions will be better positioned to stand out in a competitive market. Personalization is expected to become even more sophisticated, with the ability to predict consumers' needs before they even recognize them.

The integration of emerging technologies such as augmented reality (AR) and virtual reality (VR) is also poised to transform the customer experience. These technologies offer new ways to interact with products and services, creating even more immersive and personalized experiences. For example, a consumer can use AR to visualize how a piece of furniture will look in their home before purchasing it, increasing the likelihood of purchase.

The experience economy, driven by personalization through AI, is redefining the way companies interact with consumers. As consumers become more demanding and are willing to pay more for unique experiences, companies must adopt technologies that enable personalization at scale. Effective implementation of AI not only improves the customer experience but also provides significant opportunities for growth and profit.

Investing in personalization and AI is not just a passing trend; it is a strategic necessity for companies that want to thrive in the digital age. Those that embrace these changes will be well positioned to capture consumers' attention and create experiences that resonate deeply, ushering in a new era of loyalty and market success.

CHAPTER 18: HOW ARTIFICIAL INTELLIGENCE WILL RESHAPE THE FUTURE OF WEALTH

The Future of the AI Economy

Artificial Intelligence (AI) is quickly becoming one of the key drivers of the global economy, shaping not only existing businesses but also creating new opportunities that have the potential to generate the next generation of millionaires. With the advancement of AI technologies, the job market and economic dynamics are expected to undergo profound transformations, especially in emerging markets. By exploring how trends in AI and technology are shaping the future of wealth, we can better understand how these new rich are forming and what opportunities are emerging.

AI technologies are being applied across sectors, from healthcare to agriculture, and their ability to process large amounts of data quickly and efficiently is making them indispensable. A McKinsey Global Institute study estimates that AI could add up to $13 trillion to the global economy by 2030. This growth will not only come from established companies, but also from startups and entrepreneurs in emerging markets who are leveraging AI to create solutions. innovative and disruptive.

The Role of Emerging Markets in the New AI Economy

Emerging markets are well positioned to benefit from AI technologies as they often have fewer inhibitions when adopting new technologies. Countries such as India, Brazil and South Africa are experiencing accelerated growth in the adoption of digital technologies and AI, which is resulting in an increase in business opportunities. These markets have young, technology-hungry populations ready to engage in new business models that AI can offer.

A clear example is India, where technology startups are using AI to solve local problems, from optimizing agricultural processes to improving healthcare services. The company Niramai, for example, uses AI to offer early diagnosis of breast cancer, demonstrating how technology can positively impact people's lives and, at the same time, create new opportunities for wealth. As these emerging markets adopt AI-based solutions, we can expect to see the emergence of new millionaires who are taking advantage of these opportunities.

AI and the Creation of New Industries

The rise of AI is not only transforming existing industries, but it is also creating entire new industries. As companies look for ways to incorporate AI into their operations, new areas of expertise are emerging, such as data analysis, cybersecurity, and developing machine learning algorithms. This is resulting in an increase in demand for qualified professionals who can work in these areas, paving the way for new entrepreneurs who are willing to explore these opportunities.

An interesting example is the digital health industry,

which is expanding rapidly as AI is used to develop solutions that improve the efficiency and effectiveness of healthcare. Startups offering telemedicine services, like Teladoc, are benefiting from this trend, becoming market leaders and creating wealth opportunities for their founders and investors.

The Potential of Automation

In addition to creating new industries, AI-driven automation is reshaping the way businesses operate. With the ability to automate routine processes and tasks, companies can reduce costs and increase efficiency. This not only frees up resources for innovation, but also creates opportunities for new business models based on automated services.

For example, the manufacturing sector is seeing an increase in the use of AI-equipped robots to optimize production. These robots not only increase productivity but also reduce errors, allowing companies to offer higher quality products at more competitive prices. As automation expands, new entrepreneurs are finding ways to monetize their skills in software development and automation engineering, thus creating a new niche market that can lead to a significant increase in wealth.

The Connection between AI and Sustainability

One of the areas where AI can have a significant impact is in promoting sustainability. As the world faces environmental challenges, companies are looking for ways to become more sustainable, and AI can play a crucial role in this effort. AI solutions are being applied in sectors such as energy, transport and agriculture to optimize the use of resources and reduce the carbon footprint.

Startups that focus on sustainable technologies, such as precision agriculture, are becoming increasingly popular. Companies like Indigo Ag use AI to help farmers maximize their yields while minimizing the use of chemical inputs, creating a positive impact on the environment while opening up new profit opportunities. This intersection between technology and sustainability not only attracts investment, but also creates a new group of entrepreneurs who are standing out in the market.

The Impact of AI on Education and Training

The future of wealth will also be shaped by how AI is transforming education and job training. With automation and digitalization becoming prevalent, the need for technology skills is growing rapidly. AI can personalize learning, making it more accessible and efficient for individuals of all ages.

Online learning platforms like Coursera and edX are integrating AI to deliver personalized courses that adapt to learners' pace and needs. This means that anyone, regardless of their background, can acquire new skills and qualify for jobs that require knowledge of AI and technology. As more people become qualified, we can expect an increase in competition and innovation, resulting in the formation of new millionaires around the world.

Innovation as an Engine of Wealth

Finally, innovation will be a crucial driver of wealth creation in the future. As AI continues to evolve, new solutions and services will be developed to meet the changing needs of consumers and businesses. This dynamic creates a cycle of innovation, where those who are able to anticipate trends and offer innovative solutions will have the chance to prosper.

Startups at the forefront of AI technology, like OpenAI and DeepMind, are leading the way in terms of innovations that have the potential to revolutionize the way we interact with technology. These ventures not only attract significant investment, but also create new employment and business opportunities that can lead to the creation of new rich people.

Artificial Intelligence is poised to reshape the future of wealth in ways we are still beginning to understand. With the potential to create new industries, transform emerging markets and optimize existing processes, AI is becoming a powerful force that can generate new wealth opportunities for those willing to adapt and innovate.

As we move toward an increasingly technology-dependent future, those who take advantage of the opportunities offered by AI will be best positioned to become the new millionaires of the digital age. AI's impact on the global economy is undeniable, and its ability to shape the future of wealth is a testament to technology's transformative power in our lives.

CHAPTER 19: THE FASTEST PATH TO A MILLION: CURRENT STRATEGIES

Introduction

The pursuit of wealth is a common goal for many people. In the modern world, this desire is fueled by success stories of millionaires and billionaires who achieved their fortune through innovative and effective strategies. In this chapter, we will explore the proven tactics these successful individuals have used to build their wealth, with a special focus on the role of Artificial Intelligence (AI) and emerging technologies.

The Growth Mindset

One of the most important keys to becoming a millionaire is cultivating a growth mindset. This mindset is characterized by the willingness to learn, adapt and face challenges. Individuals like Elon Musk and Richard Branson exemplify this mindset, as they both faced significant failures before achieving success. The ability to see failures as learning opportunities is a key factor that allows people to bounce back and continue pursuing their financial goals.

Psychologist Carol Dweck, author of the book "Mindset: The New Psychology of Success," argues that people with a growth mindset are more likely to take calculated risks and seek creative solutions to problems. This willingness to learn and adapt is critical in an ever-changing world where new technologies like AI are revolutionizing industries and creating new opportunities.

The Role of Financial Education

Financial education is another crucial component on the journey to becoming a millionaire. Many successful millionaires, like Warren Buffett, emphasize the importance of understanding how money works. Investing time in learning about investing, saving, and managing money can give you a significant advantage in building wealth.

AI and digital platforms are making financial education more accessible than ever. Apps like Robinhood and Acorns help people invest in stocks and save by offering a user-friendly interface that democratizes access to the financial market. This accessibility allows more individuals to develop their financial skills, helping them make informed decisions that can lead to wealth creation.

Networking and Collaborations

Building a solid network of contacts is a strategy that many millionaires adopt to accelerate their path to riches. Effective networking is not just about meeting influential people, but also about establishing collaborative relationships that can generate business opportunities.

Individuals like Oprah Winfrey and Mark Zuckerberg have built their fortunes, in part, through collaborations and strategic partnerships. AI can facilitate this process by offering tools that connect people with similar interests. Platforms like LinkedIn and customer relationship management tools (CRMs) help maintain these connections, allowing entrepreneurs and professionals to exchange ideas and explore new opportunities.

Investing in Emerging Technologies

The most astute investors are constantly looking for new opportunities in emerging technologies. AI, blockchain, biotechnology and renewable energy are just some of the areas that are attracting significant investment and promise explosive growth potential.

Investors like Chamath Palihapitiya and Peter Thiel are known for their ability to identify and invest in innovative startups before they become mainstream. A study conducted by Crunchbase shows that startups using AI are more likely to receive significant investment, highlighting the importance of staying ahead of the technological curve.

Artificial Intelligence can also be used to analyze market trends and predict which sectors have the greatest potential for growth. Predictive analytics tools like Google Trends and data analytics platforms enable investors to make informed, data-driven decisions.

Investment Diversification

Another vital strategy for accumulating wealth is investment diversification. The idea is not to put all your eggs in one basket, minimizing risk while maximizing return potential. Many renowned millionaires and investors, such as Ray Dalio and Warren Buffett, advocate diversification as a fundamental approach to creating wealth.

AI can play a significant role in diversification by allowing investors to quickly analyze a variety of assets and sectors. With algorithms that can process large amounts of data, AI can identify investment opportunities that may not be evident at first glance. This helps investors balance their portfolios effectively while maintaining an acceptable level of risk.

Entrepreneurship and Innovation

Entrepreneurship is one of the most common routes to wealth. Many millionaires have built their fortunes by creating innovative products or services that meet a market need. Steve Jobs, for example, turned Apple into one of the most valuable companies in the world, largely due to his ability to innovate and create products that changed the way people interact with technology.

However, innovation is not just for those who have an original idea. With AI, anyone can explore entrepreneurship, whether by creating an app, developing an e-commerce website or offering services on a new digital platform. AI tools are helping entrepreneurs streamline their operations and reach a wider audience, which can result in rapid growth and, ultimately, wealth.

The Impact of Social Media

Social media has changed the way companies connect with consumers and how individuals can build their personal brands. Platforms like Instagram, TikTok and YouTube offer unparalleled opportunities to monetize skills and passions.

Digital influencers and content creators are becoming millionaires by building their personal brands and monetizing their followers. AI is playing a crucial role in optimizing digital marketing, enabling companies to analyze user data and personalize their marketing campaigns effectively.

Examples from individuals like Kylie Jenner and PewDiePie demonstrate that building an online presence can result in significant wealth. The key is understanding how to use social media to connect with an audience and create a value proposition that resonates with consumers.

The Importance of Resilience

Finally, resilience is a trait that many millionaires

share. The journey to wealth is rarely linear and is fraught with challenges and obstacles. Those who can recover from failures and continue moving forward are often the ones who achieve success.

AI can assist in this process by providing data and analysis that helps entrepreneurs learn from mistakes and adjust their business strategies. Additionally, machine learning technologies are becoming more accessible, allowing anyone to utilize these tools to adapt and thrive, regardless of circumstances.

The fastest path to becoming a millionaire in the modern world requires a combination of a growth mindset, financial education, networking, innovation and resilience. Emerging technologies, especially AI, are shaping this path, offering new opportunities and tools that can accelerate the journey to wealth.

The key to success is being willing to learn, adapt and explore the countless opportunities that the digital age offers. With a strategic approach and a willingness to harness innovation, anyone can embark on the path to riches and become the next millionaire of the modern era.

FINAL THOUGHTS: YOUR ROADMAP TO A MILLION

Throughout this book, we explore a variety of strategies and tools that can turn dreams of wealth into tangible realities. The journey to becoming a millionaire is not just a matter of luck or opportunity; It is, above all, a matter of choice and action. With the right tools and strategies, anyone can chart their own path to financial prosperity.

The Power of Strategies

What sets millionaires apart from others is their ability to consistently apply effective strategies. Each chapter in this book offered valuable insights into different aspects that contribute to financial success, from financial literacy to entrepreneurship and technological innovation. It is essential that readers not only understand these concepts, but also put them into practice in their daily lives.

Often, the simplest ideas can generate the biggest impacts. For example, automation in business may seem like a small step, but it can free up precious time and increase efficiency, allowing entrepreneurs to focus on growth strategies. Likewise, understanding the importance of networking and collaborations can open doors that previously seemed unreachable.

Turning Ideas into Action

The real challenge lies in transforming ideas into concrete actions. This is the time to act. If you've been inspired by any of the success stories or strategies discussed, now is the time to take the first step. Start small, but think big. Whether you are a beginning investor or a budding entrepreneur, action is the catalyst that begins the journey to success.

Identify an area where you can apply what you learned. It could be implementing new financial management software, launching a small online business, or joining a professional network. Every small step is progress towards your ultimate goal.

The Success Mindset

A success mindset is essential on any journey. Adopt a positive approach and stay motivated, even in the face of challenges. Resilience and the ability to learn from failures are common characteristics among those who achieve great things. Remember that every obstacle is an opportunity in disguise to grow and learn.

Furthermore, curiosity and the willingness to continue learning are essential. The world is constantly changing, and the ability to adapt and evolve with new trends and technologies is crucial to long-term success. Emotional intelligence also plays a vital role as the ability to manage emotions and relationships can directly influence your business opportunities.

Celebrating Success

As you progress on your journey, don't forget to celebrate your achievements, no matter how small. Every milestone achieved is a testament to your dedication and effort. This not only reinforces your motivation, but also serves as a reminder that success is an ongoing and cumulative process.

Finally, remember that millionaire status is more than just numbers on a bank statement; it's about freedom, opportunities, and the ability to positively impact other people's lives. As you build your wealth, consider how you can use your resources to make a difference in the world around you.

Conclusion

The conclusion of this book is not an end, but a new beginning. With the knowledge acquired and the determination to act, you have the map to the million in your hands. Financial success is within your reach; all you have to do is take the first step. So, go ahead, apply the concepts discussed and start turning your ideas into action. The path to wealth is full of possibilities — and now, with the right tools and strategies, you are prepared to take this journey.

www.ingramcontent.com/pod-product-compliance
Lightning Source LLC
Chambersburg PA
CBHW050322230526
45471CB00005B/2311